DIABETIC Cooking FOR 1 OR 2

Cooking for 1 or 2

Cooking for just yourself or yourself and one other person has many challenges. Most recipes make 4 or more servings. That means you may be tempted to eat more than one serving. Or, you must deal with leftovers tomorrow. Sometimes it just seems easier to buy a frozen meal, eat carry-out food, or even fast food. For people with diabetes every meal is important and the challenge to make it a healthy one is always present. *Diabetic Cooking for 1 or 2* is the perfect solution to these problems.

Quick & Easy Dinners

In the **"Quick & Easy Dinners"** chapter, you'll find a delightful assortment of recipes, some for just one and many for two. All of the recipes are suitable for everyday meals. From soups and stews to casseroles and stir-fries, you'll find lots of choices. These recipes can easily be doubled for those occasions when you need to serve more.

5 Ingredients or Less

The **"5 Ingredients or Less"** chapter was designed for those who don't have much time to spend cooking or those looking for extra-easy meals. Not included in the five ingredients are salt, pepper, water, cooking oil or nonstick cooking spray—items you have on hand. You'll be amazed just how delicious five ingredients can be.

Fabulous Flavors

"Fabulous Flavors" offers you delicious recipes with bold flavors. You'll find taste-intensive Jamaican Jerk Turkey Wraps, Thai Curry Stir-Fry and Southwest Roasted Salmon & Corn. Say goodbye to bland and boring meals.

Meatless Meals

The **"Meatless Meals"** chapter offers you the choice of a lower-protein meal. These recipes are also suitable for a dinner guest who is vegetarian. If you need more protein, simply add two or three ounces of lean chicken, turkey, fish or meat.

2 Cooking for 1 or 2

When a sugar-free packaged cookie just won't do, choose a fabulously easy dessert from **"Delicious Desserts."** Some have no sugar added and others use small amounts of sugar. Carbohydrate contents range from 15 to 37 grams.

Cooking Equipment

Most of the recipes in this publication require the same skillets and saucepans that you use every day. Some of the recipes call for small casserole or baking dishes (1½ cups to 1½ quarts). If you don't have these, look for inexpensive 4-cup and 6-cup ovenproof, microwavable glass storage containers (available at supermarkets or mass merchandisers). Large custard cups, individual soufflé dishes, and 7×5-inch baking dishes and small gratin dishes are also excellent choices. A great source for small casserole, soufflé and gratin dishes is garage or yard sales. Unless they are marked as microwave-safe, use these dishes only in a conventional oven. A small scale can be a useful, but not necessary, tool for weighing fruits, vegetables and small amounts of pasta.

About the Recipes

The recipes in *Diabetic Cooking for 1 or 2* were specifically developed for people with diabetes. All are based on the principals of sound nutrition as outlined by the dietary guidelines developed by the United States Department of Agriculture and the United States Department of Health and Human Services, making them perfect for the entire family.

Although the recipes are not intended as a medically therapeutic program, nor as a substitute for medically approved meal plans for individuals with diabetes, they contain amounts of calories, fat, cholesterol, sodium and carbohydrate that will fit easily into an individualized meal plan designed by your physician, certified diabetes educator or registered dietitian, and you.

The goal of this publication is to provide a variety of recipes suitable for people with diabetes. Since diabetic meal plans can vary from one individual to another, not all recipes may be suitable for every person with diabetes. Therefore, each individual must choose wisely from among the recipes in this book based on information provided by your physician, certified diabetes educator, registered dietitian, and your past experience.

A Few Words about Sugar

In 1994, the American Diabetes Association lifted the absolute ban on sugar from the recommended dietary guidelines for people with diabetes. Under updated guidelines, you can, for example, exchange 1 tablespoon of sugar for a slice of bread because each is considered a starch exchange. The new guidelines for sugar intake are based on scientific studies that show that carbohydrate in the form of sugars do not raise blood glucose levels more rapidly that other types of carbohydrate-containing food. What is more important is the total amount of carbohydrate eaten, not the source.

However, keep in mind that sweets and other foods high in sugar are usually high in calories and fat and contain few, if any, other nutrients, so the choice between an apple and a doughnut is still an easy one to make. Nobody, diabetic or not, should be eating foods filled with lots of sugar. But, when calculated into the nutritional analysis, a small amount of sugar can enhance a recipe and will not be harmful.

If you have any questions or concerns about incorporating sugar into your daily meal plans, consult your physician and certified diabetes educator or registered dietitian for more information.

Nutritional Analysis

The nutritional analysis that appears with each recipe was calculated by an independent nutritional consulting firm. Every effort has been made to check the accuracy of these numbers. However, because numerous variables account for a wide range of values in certain foods, all analyses that appear in this publication should be considered approximate.

♦ The analysis of each recipe includes all the ingredients that are listed in that recipe, except those labeled as "optional." Nutritional analysis is provided for the primary recipe only, not the recipe variations.

♦ If a range of amounts is offered for an ingredient (1 to 1¼ cups), the first amount given was used to calculate the nutritional information.

♦ If an ingredient is presented with an option ("1 cup hot cooked rice or noodles" for example), the first item listed was used to calculate the nutritional information.

♦ Foods shown in photographs on the same serving plate or offered as "serving suggestions" at the end of the recipe are not included in the recipe analysis unless they are listed in the ingredient list.

♦ In recipes calling for cooked rice or pasta or calling for rice or pasta to be cooked according to package directions, the analysis was based on preparation without salt and fat unless otherwise stated in the recipe.

Quick & EASY DINNERS

Seafood & Vegetable Stir-Fry

2 teaspoons olive oil
½ medium red or yellow bell
  pepper, cut into strips
½ medium onion, cut into
  small wedges
10 snow peas, trimmed and
  cut diagonally into
  halves

1 clove garlic, minced
6 ounces frozen cooked
  medium shrimp, thawed
2 tablespoons stir-fry sauce
1 cup hot cooked rice

1. Heat oil in large nonstick skillet over medium-high heat. Add vegetables; stir-fry 4 minutes. Add garlic; stir fry 1 minute or until vegetables are crisp-tender.

2. Add shrimp and stir-fry sauce. Stir-fry 1 to 2 minutes or until hot. Serve over rice. *Makes 2 servings*

Nutrients per Serving: Calories: 279, Calories from Fat: 19%, Total Fat: 6 g, Saturated Fat: 1 g, Protein: 22 g, Carbohydrate: 33 g, Cholesterol: 166 mg, Sodium: 724 mg, Fiber: 2 g, Iron: 2 mg, Calcium: 69 mg, Vitamin A: 73 RE, Vitamin C: 43 mg, Sugar: 4 g
Dietary Exchanges: 2 Vegetable, 1½ Starch, 2 Meat

Seafood & Vegetable Stir-Fry

Chicken & Orzo Soup

Nonstick olive oil cooking spray

3 ounces boneless skinless chicken breast, cut into bite-size pieces

1 can (about 14 ounces) fat-free, reduced-sodium chicken broth

1 cup water

⅔ cup shredded carrot

⅓ cup sliced green onion

¼ cup uncooked orzo pasta

1 teaspoon grated fresh ginger

⅛ teaspoon ground turmeric

2 teaspoons lemon juice

Black pepper

Sliced green onions (optional)

1. Spray medium saucepan with cooking spray. Heat over medium-high heat. Add chicken. Cook and stir 2 to 3 minutes or until no longer pink. Remove from saucepan and set aside.

2. In same saucepan combine broth, water, carrot, onion, orzo, ginger and turmeric. Bring to a boil. Reduce heat and simmer, covered, 8 to 10 minutes or until orzo is tender. Stir in chicken and lemon juice; cook until hot. Season to taste with pepper.

3. Ladle into serving bowls. Sprinkle with green onions, if desired.

Makes 2 servings

Tip: Orzo is a tiny rice-shaped pasta. If it is not available, substitute any very small pasta.

Nutrients per Serving: Calories: 176, Calories from Fat: 8%, Total Fat: 2 g, Saturated Fat: <1 g, Protein: 18 g, Carbohydrate: 21 g, Cholesterol: 26 mg, Sodium: 182 mg, Fiber: 2 g, Iron: 2 mg, Calcium: 38 mg, Vitamin A: 1036 RE, Vitamin C: 8 mg, Sugar: 4 g
Dietary Exchanges: 1 Vegetable, 1 Starch, 1½ Meat

Chicken & Orzo Soup

Spicy Black Bean & Sausage Stew

1 tablespoon olive oil
½ cup chopped onion
¼ cup chopped green bell pepper
4 ounces low-fat smoked sausage, cut into ¼-inch pieces
2 cloves garlic, minced
1 cup drained canned black beans, rinsed
¾ cup undrained no-salt-added stewed tomatoes
1½ teaspoons dried oregano leaves
¾ teaspoon ground cumin
2 tablespoons minced fresh parsley
Hot pepper sauce
Hot cooked rice (optional)

1. Heat oil in medium skillet over medium heat. Add onion, bell pepper and sausage. Cook and stir 3 to 4 minutes or until vegetables are tender. Add garlic; cook and stir 1 minute.

2. Stir in beans, tomatoes with juice, oregano and cumin, breaking up tomatoes into small chunks. Bring to a boil; reduce heat to low. Cover and simmer 20 minutes, stirring occasionally. Stir in parsley and pepper sauce to taste. Serve with hot cooked rice, if desired.

Makes 2 servings

Serving Suggestion: Top each serving with a mound of ¼ cup hot cooked rice, if desired. This will add 67 calories and 14 grams carbohydrate to each serving.

Tip: High fiber foods make you feel fuller and are a great way to control hunger. They may also lower total cholesterol and low density lipoprotein (LDL). LDL is often referred to as "bad" cholesterol.

Nutrients per Serving: Calories: 266, Calories from Fat: 30%, Total Fat: 11 g, Saturated Fat: 2 g, Protein: 16 g, Carbohydrate: 39 g, Cholesterol: 26 mg, Sodium: 1022 mg, Fiber: 10 g, Iron: 4 mg, Calcium: 131 mg, Vitamin A: 70 RE, Vitamin C: 50 mg, Sugar: 10 g
Dietary Exchanges: 1 Vegetable, 2 Starch, 2 Fat

Spicy Black Bean & Sausage Stew

Baked Orange Roughy with Sautéed Vegetables

2 orange roughy fillets
(about 4 ounces each)
2 teaspoons olive oil
1 medium carrot, cut into
matchstick pieces
4 medium mushrooms, sliced

⅓ cup chopped onion
¼ cup chopped green or
yellow bell pepper
1 clove garlic, minced
Black pepper
Lemon wedges

1. Preheat oven to 350°F. Place fish fillets in shallow baking dish. Bake 15 minutes or until fish flakes easily when tested with fork.

2. Heat olive oil in small nonstick skillet over medium-high heat. Add carrots; cook 3 minutes, stirring occasionally. Add mushrooms, onion, bell pepper and garlic; cook and stir 2 minutes or until vegetables are crisp-tender.

3. Place fish on serving plates; top with vegetable mixture. Sprinkle with black pepper. Serve with lemon wedges.

Makes 2 servings

Note: To microwave fish, place fish in shallow microwavable dish. Microwave, covered, on HIGH 2 minutes or until fish flakes easily when tested with fork. To broil fish, place fish on rack of broiler pan. Broil 4 to 6 inches from heat 4 minutes on each side or until fish flakes easily when tested with fork.

Nutrients per Serving: Calories: 157, Calories from Fat: 32%, Total Fat: 6 g, Saturated Fat: 1 g, Protein: 18 g, Carbohydrate: 10 g, Cholesterol: 22 mg, Sodium: 84 mg, Fiber: 3 g, Iron: 1 mg, Calcium: 54 mg, Vitamin A: 1050, Vitamin C: 32 mg, Sugar: 4 g
Dietary Exchanges: 1½ Vegetable, 2 Meat

Meatballs in Creamy Mustard Sauce

6 ounces 95% lean ground
    beef sirloin
⅓ cup fresh bread crumbs
2 tablespoons chopped
    green onion with tops
1 tablespoon plus
    1 teaspoon Dijon
    mustard, divided
½ teaspoon lemon pepper
¼ teaspoon salt

3 ounces uncooked fettuccine
    or 1¼ cups tri-color
    rotini pasta
½ cup fat-free reduced-
    sodium beef broth
2 teaspoons cornstarch
3 tablespoons reduced-fat
    sour cream
Minced fresh parsley
    (optional)

1. Preheat oven to 400°F. Spray broiler pan with nonstick cooking spray.

2. Combine beef, bread crumbs, green onion, 1 tablespoon mustard, lemon pepper and salt in small bowl. Shape into 8 meatballs. Place in single layer on prepared broiler pan. Bake, uncovered, 15 minutes or until no longer pink in center.

3. Meanwhile, cook fettucine in medium saucepan according to package directions. Drain and keep warm

4. Whisk together beef broth, remaining 1 teaspoon mustard and cornstarch in same saucepan until smooth. Cook over low heat, stirring constantly, until mixture comes to a boil. Remove from heat. Stir about 1 tablespoon broth mixture into sour cream. Stir sour cream mixture into broth mixture in saucepan. Heat over low heat 1 minute. *Do not boil.* Remove from heat; stir in meatballs. Serve immediately.

5. Divide fettuccine between two serving plates and top with meatballs and sauce. Sprinkle with parsley, if desired.

Makes 2 servings

Nutrients per Serving: Calories: 318, Calories from Fat: 23%, Total Fat: 8 g, Saturated Fat: 3 g, Protein: 24 g, Carbohydrate: 37 g, Cholesterol: 52 mg, Sodium: 657 mg, Fiber: 2 g, Iron: 3 mg, Calcium: 72 mg, Vitamin A: 32 RE, Vitamin C: 7 mg, Sugar: 3 g
Dietary Exchanges: 2½ Starch, 2½ Meat

Bacon-Wrapped Scallops on Angel Hair Pasta

1 reduced-sodium bacon slice, cut crosswise into thirds

3 sea scallops (2 ounces)

2 ounces uncooked angel hair pasta

1 tablespoon reduced-fat margarine

2 green onions with tops, sliced

1 small clove garlic, minced

Black pepper or garlic pepper, to taste

1. Wrap one bacon piece around each scallop; secure with toothpick.

2. Cook pasta according to package directions. Drain pasta; return to pan.

3. Meanwhile, heat small nonstick skillet over medium heat. Add scallops; cook 2 to 3 minutes on each side or until bacon is crisp and scallops are opaque. Remove scallops from skillet; discard toothpicks. Reduce heat to low.

4. Melt margarine in same skillet.* Add onion and garlic; cook and stir 1 minute or until onion is tender. Remove from heat.

5. Add onion mixture to pasta; toss lightly. Place on serving plate. Top with scallops. Season with pepper.   *Makes 1 serving*

*If there are enough drippings in the skillet after the bacon is cooked, you may not need the margarine for cooking the onion and garlic. Without the margarine, calories are 245, total fat is 4 grams and the percentage of fat is 15.

Nutrients per Serving: Calories: 305, Calories from Fat: 32%, Total Fat: 11 g, Saturated Fat: 2 g, Protein: 20 g, Carbohydrate: 32 g, Cholesterol: 93 mg, Sodium: 328 mg, Fiber: 2 g, Iron: 3 mg, Calcium: 73 mg, Vitamin A: 113 RE, Vitamin C: 3 mg, Sugar: 1 g
Dietary Exchanges: 2 Starch, 2 Meat, 1 Fat

Bacon-Wrapped Scallops on Angel Hair Pasta

Curried Chicken Pot Pies

1 tablespoon canola oil
¾ cup chopped peeled
   Granny Smith apple
⅓ cup thinly sliced carrot
¼ cup chopped onion
1 clove garlic, minced
1 tablespoon flour
½ teaspoon curry powder
⅛ teaspoon salt
⅛ teaspoon black pepper
   Pinch ground cloves
¾ cup water

1 cup chopped cooked
   chicken breast
½ cup no-salt-added diced
   tomatoes, undrained
2 tablespoons minced fresh
   cilantro
4 refrigerated soft
   breadsticks (⅔ of 7-
   ounce can)
Additional minced fresh
   cilantro (optional)

1. Preheat oven to 375°F. Spray two 1½-cup casseroles or ovenproof bowls with nonstick cooking spray.

2. Heat oil in medium skillet over medium heat. Add apple, carrot, onion and garlic. Cook and stir 3 to 4 minutes or until apple and onion are tender. Add flour, curry powder, salt, pepper and cloves. Cook and stir over medium heat 1 minute. Stir in water. Cook, stirring constantly, until liquid boils and thickens. Stir in chicken and tomatoes. Cook 3 to 4 minutes or until heated through. Stir in 2 tablespoons cilantro. Spoon into prepared casseroles.

3. Arrange 2 breadsticks over top of chicken mixture in each casserole. Sprinkle additional cilantro over tops, if desired.

4. Bake 15 to 17 minutes or until breadsticks are browned and filling is bubbly.   *Makes 2 servings*

Note: Leftover breadstick dough may be refrigerated in an airtight container and reserved for another use.

Nutrients per Serving: Calories: 491, Calories from Fat: 29%, Total Fat: 16 g, Saturated Fat: 3 g, Protein: 29 g, Carbohydrate: 57 g, Cholesterol: 60 mg, Sodium: 794 mg, Fiber: 4 g, Iron: 4 mg, Calcium: 53 mg, Vitamin A: 573, Vitamin C: 17 mg, Sugar: 15 g
Dietary Exchanges: 1 Fruit, 3 Starch, 2 Meat, 2 Fat

Curried Chicken Pot Pie

Grilled Salsa Turkey Burger

3 ounces lean ground turkey
1 tablespoon mild or
   medium salsa
1 tablespoon crushed baked
   tortilla chips
1 (1-ounce) reduced-fat
   Monterey Jack cheese
   slice (optional)

1 whole wheat hamburger
   bun, split
1 lettuce leaf
   Additional salsa

1. Combine turkey, 1 tablespoon salsa and chips in small bowl; mix lightly. Shape into patty. Lightly oil grid or broiler rack to prevent sticking.

2. Grill over medium-hot coals or broil 4 to 6 inches from heat 6 minutes on each side or until no longer pink in center, turning once. Top with cheese during last 2 minutes of grilling time, if desired. Place bun, cut sides down, on grill during last 2 minutes of grilling time to toast until lightly browned.

3. Cover bottom half of bun with lettuce; top with burger, additional salsa and top half of bun. *Makes 1 serving*

Tip: When purchasing ground turkey, check the package label to be sure it contains only white meat. Ground turkey with dark meat and skin may be high in fat. Choose turkey that is at least 97% lean.

Nutrients per Serving: Calories: 302, Calories from Fat: 33%, Total Fat: 11 g, Saturated Fat: 3 g, Protein: 22 g, Carbohydrate: 10 g, Cholesterol: 63 mg, Sodium: 494 mg, Fiber: 2 g, Iron: 3 mg, Calcium: 88 mg, Vitamin A: 20 RE, Vitamin C: 2 mg, Sugar: 4 g
Dietary Exchanges: 2 Starch, 2 Meat, 1 Fat

Baked Pasta Casserole

1½ cups (3 ounces) uncooked wagon wheel or rotelle pasta

3 ounces 95% lean ground beef sirloin

2 tablespoons chopped onion

2 tablespoons chopped green bell pepper

1 clove garlic, minced

½ cup fat-free spaghetti sauce

Black pepper

2 tablespoons shredded Italian-style mozzarella and Parmesan cheese blend

Pepperoncini (optional)

1. Preheat oven to 350°F. Cook pasta according to package directions; drain. Return pasta to saucepan.

2. Meanwhile, heat small nonstick skillet over medium-high heat. Add beef, onion, bell pepper and garlic; cook and stir 3 to 4 minutes or until beef is browned and vegetables are crisp-tender. Drain.

3. Add beef mixture, spaghetti sauce and black pepper to pasta in saucepan; mix well. Spoon mixture into 1 quart baking dish. Sprinkle with cheese.

4. Bake 15 minutes or until heated through. Serve with pepperoncini, if desired. *Makes 2 servings*

Note: To make ahead, assemble casserole as directed above through step 3. Cover and refrigerate several hours or overnight. Bake, uncovered, in preheated 350°F oven for 30 minutes or until heated through.

Nutrients per Serving: Calories: 282, Calories from Fat: 23%, Total Fat: 7 g, Saturated Fat: 3 g, Protein: 16 g, Carbohydrate: 37 g, Cholesterol: 31 mg, Sodium: 368 mg, Fiber: 3 g, Iron: 3 mg, Calcium: 36 mg, Vitamin A: 49 RE, Vitamin C: 17 mg, Sugar: 5 g
Dietary Exchanges: 2 Vegetable, 2 Starch, 1 Meat, 1 Fat

Tilapia & Sweet Corn Baked in Parchment

⅔ cup fresh or frozen corn kernels

¼ cup finely chopped onion

¼ cup finely chopped red bell pepper

2 cloves garlic, minced

1 teaspoon chopped fresh rosemary *or* ½ teaspoon crushed dried rosemary, divided

½ teaspoon salt, divided

¼ to ½ teaspoon black pepper, divided

2 tilapia fillets (4 ounces each)

1 teaspoon olive oil

1. Preheat oven to 400°F. Cut two 15-inch squares of parchment paper; fold each piece in half.

2. Combine corn, onion, bell pepper, garlic, ½ teaspoon fresh rosemary, ¼ teaspoon salt and half the black pepper in small bowl. Open parchment paper; spoon half the corn mixture on one side of each piece, spreading out slightly.

3. Arrange tilapia fillets on top of corn mixture. Brush fish with oil; sprinkle with remaining ½ teaspoon fresh rosemary, ¼ teaspoon salt and black pepper.

4. To seal packets, fold other half of parchment over fish and corn. Fold and crimp along edges until completely sealed. Place packets on baking sheet.

5. Bake 15 minutes or until fish is opaque throughout. Remove packets to serving plates. Carefully cut open centers of packets and peel back paper. *Makes 2 servings*

Note: Heavy-duty foil may be substituted for the parchment paper. To serve, remove fish and corn from foil.

Nutrients per Serving: Calories: 189, Calories from Fat: 21%, Total Fat: 5 g, Saturated Fat: <1 g, Protein: 24 g, Carbohydrate: 15 g, Cholesterol: 0 mg, Sodium: 622 mg, Fiber: 2 g, Iron: 1 mg, Calcium: 46 mg, Vitamin A: 40 RE, Vitamin C: 13 mg, Sugar: 2 g
Dietary Exchanges: 1 Starch, 3 Meat

Tilapia & Sweet Corn Baked in Parchment

Crustless Salmon & Broccoli Quiche

¾ cup cholesterol-free egg substitute

¼ cup plain nonfat yogurt

¼ cup chopped green onions with tops

2 teaspoons all-purpose flour

1 teaspoon dried basil leaves

⅛ teaspoon salt

⅛ teaspoon black pepper

¾ cup frozen broccoli florets, thawed and drained

⅓ cup (3 ounces) drained and flaked water-packed boneless, skinless canned salmon

2 tablespoons grated Parmesan cheese

1 plum tomato, thinly sliced

¼ cup fresh bread crumbs

1. Preheat oven to 375°F. Spray 6-cup rectangular casserole or 9-inch pie plate with nonstick cooking spray.

2. Combine egg substitute, yogurt, green onions, flour, basil, salt and pepper in medium bowl until well blended. Stir in broccoli, salmon and Parmesan cheese. Spread evenly in prepared casserole. Top with tomato slices. Sprinkle bread crumbs over top.

3. Bake 20 to 25 minutes or until knife inserted into center comes out clean. Let stand 5 minutes before serving.

Makes 2 servings

Tip: To make fresh bread crumbs, remove the crusts from bread slices and tear bread into small pieces. Use any kind of bread, but day-old French and Italian bread make the best bread crumbs.

Nutrients per Serving: Calories: 227, Calories from Fat: 22%, Total Fat: 6 g, Saturated Fat: 2 g, Protein: 25 g, Carbohydrate: 20 g, Cholesterol: 25 mg, Sodium: 717 mg, Fiber: 5 g, Iron: 4 mg, Calcium: 307 mg, Vitamin A: 193 RE, Vitamin C: 20 mg, Sugar: 5 g
Dietary Exchanges: 1 Vegetable, 1 Starch, 2 Meat, ½ Fat

Grilled Chicken with Spicy Black Beans & Rice

1 boneless skinless chicken breast (about 4 ounces)
½ teaspoon jerk seasonings
½ teaspoon olive oil
¼ cup finely diced green bell pepper
2 teaspoons minced dried chipotle peppers
¾ cup hot cooked rice
½ cup canned rinsed and drained black beans

2 tablespoons diced pimiento
1 tablespoon chopped pimiento-stuffed green olives
1 tablespoon chopped onion
1 tablespoon chopped fresh cilantro (optional)
Lime wedges

1. Rub chicken with jerk seasonings. Grill over medium hot coals 8 to 10 minutes or until no longer pink in center.

2. Meanwhile, heat oil in medium saucepan or skillet over medium heat. Add bell pepper and chipotle pepper; cook 7 to 8 minutes, stirring frequently, until peppers are soft.

3. Add rice, beans, pimiento and olives to saucepan. Cook until hot, about 3 minutes.

4. Serve bean mixture with chicken. Top bean mixture with onion and cilantro, if desired. Garnish with lime wedges.

Makes 2 servings

Tip: Chipotle peppers are dried, smoked jalapeño peppers. They have a wrinkled, dark brown skin and a smokey sweet flavor.

Nutrients per Serving: Calories: 214, Calories from Fat: 18%, Total Fat: 5 g, Saturated Fat: 1 g, Protein: 17 g, Carbohydrate: 30 g, Cholesterol: 34 mg, Sodium: 436 mg, Fiber: 5 g, Iron: 2 mg, Calcium: 39 mg, Vitamin A: 55 RE, Vitamin C: 47 mg, Sugar: 2 g
Dietary Exchanges: 2 Starch, 1½ Meat

Bolognese Sauce & Penne Pasta

8 ounces ground beef sirloin
⅓ cup chopped onion
1 clove garlic, minced
1 can (8 ounces) tomato
    sauce
⅓ cup chopped carrot
¼ cup water

2 tablespoons red wine
1 teaspoon dried Italian
    seasonings
1½ cups hot cooked penne
    pasta
Chopped fresh parsley

1. Heat medium saucepan over medium heat until hot. Add beef, onion and garlic; cook and stir 5 to 7 minutes, breaking up meat with spoon, until beef is browned.

2. Add tomato sauce, carrot, water, wine and Italian seasoning. Bring to a boil. Reduce heat and simmer 15 minutes. Serve sauce over pasta. Sprinkle with parsley.   *Makes 2 servings*

Tip: Carrots add sweetness that reduces the acidic flavor of this quick bolognese sauce.

Nutrients per Serving: Calories: 292, Calories from Fat: 14%, Total Fat: 5 g, Saturated Fat: 2 g, Protein: 21 g, Carbohydrate: 40 g, Cholesterol: 45 mg, Sodium: 734 mg, Fiber: 4 g, Iron: 5 mg, Calcium: 46 mg, Vitamin A: 458 RE, Vitamin C: 23 mg, Sugar: 7 g
Dietary Exchanges: 1 Vegetable, 2 Starch, 2 Meat

Speedy Tacos

4 ounces ground beef sirloin
¼ cup chopped onion
1 clove garlic, minced
⅓ cup no-salt-added tomato
    sauce
1 tablespoon taco
    seasonings
6 taco shells

¼ cup (2 ounces) shredded
    reduced-fat Cheddar
    cheese
½ cup shredded lettuce
⅓ cup chopped tomato
¼ cup chopped onion
Hot pepper sauce
    (optional)

1. Heat small skillet over medium heat until hot. Add beef, onion and garlic; cook and stir 5 minutes until beef is browned, breaking up meat with spoon. Add tomato sauce and seasonings; cook 5 minutes.

2. Warm taco shells in oven following package directions.

3. Fill taco shells with meat mixture, cheese, lettuce, tomato and onion. Serve with pepper sauce, if desired.

Makes 2 servings (3 tacos each)

Tip: If you wish to reduce the fat in these easy tacos, simply divide the filling among four taco shells instead of six.

Nutrients per Serving: Calories: 342, Calories from Fat: 36%, Total Fat: 14 g, Saturated Fat: 4 g, Protein: 19 g, Carbohydrate: 36 g, Cholesterol: 40 mg, Sodium: 706 mg, Fiber: 5 g, Iron: 3 mg, Calcium: 211 mg, Vitamin A: 153 RE, Vitamin C: 15 mg, Sugar: 5 g
Dietary Exchanges: 1 Vegetable, 2 Starch, 2 Meat, 1½ Fat

5 Ingredients or LESS

Ravioli with Tomato Pesto

4 ounces frozen cheese
   ravioli
1¼ cups coarsely chopped
   plum tomatoes
¼ cup fresh basil leaves
2 teaspoons pine nuts

2 teaspoons olive oil
¼ teaspoon salt
⅛ teaspoon black pepper
1 tablespoon grated
   Parmesan cheese

1. Cook ravioli according to package directions; drain.

2. Meanwhile, combine tomatoes, basil, pine nuts, oil, salt and pepper in food processor. Process using on/off pulsing action just until ingredients are chopped. Serve over ravioli. Top with cheese.

Makes 2 servings

Nutrients per Serving: Calories: 175, Calories from Fat: 34%, Total Fat: 10 g, Saturated Fat: 2 g, Protein: 10 g, Carbohydrate: 20 g, Cholesterol: 59 mg, Sodium: 459 mg, Fiber: 3 g, Iron: 2 mg, Calcium: 119 mg, Vitamin A: 116 RE, Vitamin C: 27 mg, Sugar: 5 g
Dietary Exchanges: 1 Vegetable, 1 Starch, 1 Meat, ½ Fat

Ravioli with Tomato Pesto

Grilled Tropical Shrimp

¼ cup barbecue sauce
2 tablespoons pineapple
   juice or orange juice
10 ounces medium shrimp in
   shells

2 medium firm nectarines
1 yellow onion, cut into
   8 wedges. or 6 green
   onions, cut into 2-inch
   lengths

1. Stir together barbecue sauce and pineapple juice. Set aside.

2. Peel and devein shrimp. Cut each nectarine into 6 wedges. Thread shrimp, nectarines and onion wedges onto 4 long metal skewers.

3. Spray grill grid with nonstick cooking spray. Prepare grill for direct grilling. Grill skewers over medium coals 4 to 5 minutes or until shrimp are opaque, turning once and brushing frequently with barbecue sauce.   *Makes 2 servings*

Tip: Although shrimp are high in cholesterol, they are naturally low in total fat and saturated fat, making them a good choice for a low-fat diet.

Nutrients per Serving: Calories: 232, Calories from Fat: 7%, Total Fat: 2 g, Saturated Fat: <1 g, Protein: 25 g, Carbohydrate: 30 g, Cholesterol: 217 mg, Sodium: 712mg mg, Fiber: 3 g, Iron: 4 mg, Calcium: 66 mg, Vitamin A: 222 RE, Vitamin C: 15 mg, Sugar: 22 g
Dietary Exchanges: 1½ Fruit, 2½ Meat

Grilled Tropical Shrimp

Spicy Caribbean Pork Medallions

6 ounces pork tenderloin
1 teaspoon Caribbean jerk
   seasoning
Nonstick olive oil cooking
   spray

⅓ cup pineapple juice
1 teaspoon brown mustard
½ teaspoon cornstarch

1. Cut tenderloin into ½-inch-thick slices. Place each slice between 2 pieces of plastic wrap. Pound to ¼-inch thickness. Rub both sides of pork pieces with jerk seasoning.

2. Lightly spray large nonstick skillet with cooking spray; heat over medium heat until hot. Add pork. Cook 2 to 3 minutes or until no longer pink, turning once. Remove from skillet. Keep warm.

3. Stir together pineapple juice, mustard and cornstarch until smooth. Add to skillet. Cook and stir over medium heat until mixture comes to a boil and thickens slightly. Spoon over pork.

Makes 2 servings

Nutrients per Serving: Calories: 134, Calories from Fat: 23%, Total Fat: 3 g, Saturated Fat: 1 g, Protein: 18 g, Carbohydrate: 7 g, Cholesterol: 49 mg, Sodium: 319 mg, Fiber: <1 g, Iron: 1 mg, Calcium: 14 mg, Vitamin A: 1 RE, Vitamin C: 5 mg, Sugar: 5 g
Dietary Exchanges: ½ Fruit, 2 Meat

Spicy Caribbean Pork Medallions

Easy Moo Shu Pork

7 ounces pork tenderloin
Nonstick olive oil cooking
spray
4 green onions, cut into
½-inch pieces
2 tablespoons hoisin sauce
or Asian plum sauce

1½ cups packaged cole slaw
mix
4 (8-inch) fat-free flour
tortillas, warmed

1. Thinly slice pork. Lightly spray large nonstick skillet with cooking spray. Heat over medium-high heat. Add pork and green onions; stir-fry 2 to 3 minutes or until pork is no longer pink. Stir in hoisin sauce. Stir in cole slaw mix.

2. Spoon pork mixture onto tortillas. Wrap to enclose. Serve immediately. *Makes 2 servings*

Note: To warm tortillas, stack and wrap loosely in plastic wrap. Microwave on HIGH for 15 to 20 seconds or until hot and pliable.

Nutrients per Serving: Calories: 293, Calories from Fat: 13%, Total Fat: 4 g, Saturated Fat: 1 g, Protein: 26 g, Carbohydrate: 37 g, Cholesterol: 58 mg, Sodium: 672 mg, Fiber: 14 g, Iron: 1 mg, Calcium: 73 mg, Vitamin A: 396 RE, Vitamin C: 17 mg, Sugar: 3 g
Dietary Exchanges: 1 Vegetable, 2 Starch, 2 Meat

Grilled Portobello Mushroom Sandwich

1 large portobello
   mushroom, cleaned and
   stem removed
¼ medium green bell pepper,
   halved
1 thin slice red onion
1 whole wheat hamburger
   bun, split

2 tablespoons fat-free Italian
   dressing
1 (1-ounce) reduced-fat
   part-skim mozzarella
   cheese slice, cut in half

1. Brush mushroom, bell pepper, onion and cut sides of bun with some dressing; set bun aside. Place vegetables over medium-hot coals. Grill 2 minutes.

2. Turn vegetables over; brush with dressing. Grill 2 minutes or until vegetables are tender. Remove bell pepper and onion from grill.

3. Place bun halves on grill. Turn mushroom top side up; brush with any remaining dressing and cover with cheese, if desired. Grill 1 minute or until cheese is melted and bun is lightly toasted.

4. Cut pepper into strips. Place mushroom on bottom half of bun; top with pepper strips and onion slice. Cover with top half of bun.

Makes 1 serving

Note: To broil, brush mushroom, bell pepper, onion and cut sides of bun with dressing. Place vegetables on greased rack of broiler pan; set bun aside. Broil vegetables 4 to 6 inches from heat 3 minutes; turn over. Brush with dressing. Broil 3 minutes or until vegetables are tender. Place mushroom, top side up, on broiler pan; top with cheese. Place bun, cut sides up, on broiler pan. Broil 1 minute or until cheese is melted and bun is toasted. Assemble sandwich as directed above.

Nutrients per Serving: Calories: 225, Calories from Fat: 22%, Total Fat: 6 g, Saturated Fat: 3 g, Protein: 15 g, Carbohydrate: 30 g, Cholesterol: 27 mg, Sodium: 729 mg, Fiber: 6 g, Iron: 1 mg, Calcium: 337 mg, Vitamin A: 73 RE, Vitamin C: 18 mg, Sugar: 4 g
Dietary Exchanges: 2 Starch, 1 Meat, ½ Fat

Spiced Turkey with Fruit Salsa

6 ounces turkey breast
    tenderloin
2 teaspoons lime juice
1 teaspoon mesquite
    seasoning blend or
    ground cumin

½ cup frozen pitted sweet
    cherries, thawed and cut
    into halves*
¼ cup chunky salsa

*Drained canned sweet cherries may be substituted for frozen cherries.

1. Prepare grill for direct grilling. Brush both sides of turkey with lime juice. Sprinkle with mesquite seasoning.

2. Grill turkey over medium coals 15 to 20 minutes or until turkey is no longer pink in center and juices run clear, turning once.

3. Meanwhile, stir together cherries and salsa.

4. Thinly slice turkey. Spoon salsa mixture over turkey.

Makes 2 servings

Nutrients per Serving: Calories: 125, Calories from Fat: 13%, Total Fat: 2 g, Saturated Fat: 1 g, Protein: 16 g, Carbohydrate: 11 g, Cholesterol: 34 mg, Sodium: 264 mg, Fiber: 2 g, Iron: 2 mg, Calcium: 26 mg, Vitamin A: 31 RE, Vitamin C: 3 mg, Sugar: 9 g
Dietary Exchanges: ½ Fruit, 2 Meat

Spiced Turkey with Fruit Salsa

Black Beans & Rice-Stuffed Chilies

Nonstick olive oil cooking spray
2 large poblano chili peppers
½ can (15½ ounces) black beans, drained and rinsed

½ cup cooked brown rice
⅓ cup mild or medium chunky salsa
⅓ cup shredded pepper Jack cheese or reduced-fat Cheddar cheese, divided

1. Preheat oven to 375°F. Lightly spray shallow baking pan with cooking spray.

2. Cut thin slice from one side of each pepper; chop pepper slices*. In medium saucepan cook peppers in boiling water 6 minutes. Drain and rinse with cold water. Remove and discard seeds and membranes.

3. Stir together beans, rice, salsa, chopped pepper and ¼ cup cheese. Spoon into peppers, mounding mixture. Place peppers in prepared pan. Cover with foil. Bake 12 to 15 minutes or until heated through.

4. Sprinkle with remaining cheese. Bake 2 minutes more or until cheese melts. *Makes 2 servings*

*Poblano peppers can sting and irritate the skin; wear rubber gloves when handling peppers and do not touch eyes. Wash hands after handling.

Tip: Poblano chilies are dark green medium-sized chilies that range in flavor from fairly mild to quite hot. Anaheim chilies may be substituted if you prefer a mild sweet flavor.

Nutrients per Serving: Calories: 289, Calories from Fat: 25%, Total Fat: 8 g, Saturated Fat: 4 g, Protein: 12 g, Carbohydrate: 38 g, Cholesterol: 20 mg, Sodium: 984 mg, Fiber: 10 g, Iron: 2 mg, Calcium: 181 mg, Vitamin A: 154 RE, Vitamin C: 71 mg, Sugar: 6 g
Dietary Exchanges: 1 Vegetable, 2 Starch, 1½ Fat

Black Beans & Rice-Stuffed Chili

Grilled Chicken, Rice & Veggies

3 ounces boneless skinless
chicken breast

3 tablespoons reduced-fat
Italian salad dressing,
divided

½ cup fat-free reduced-
sodium chicken broth

¼ cup uncooked rice

½ cup frozen broccoli and
carrot blend, thawed

1. Place chicken and 1 tablespoon salad dressing in resealable plastic food storage bag. Seal bag; turn to coat. Marinate in refrigerator 1 hour.

2. Remove chicken from marinade; discard marinade. Grill chicken over medium-hot coals 8 to 10 minutes or until chicken is no longer pink in center.

3. Meanwhile, bring broth to a boil in small saucepan; add rice. Cover; reduce heat and simmer 15 minutes, stirring in vegetables during last 5 minutes of cooking. Remove from heat and stir in remaining 2 tablespoons dressing. Serve with chicken.

Makes 1 serving

Tip: A marinade that has been in contact with raw chicken should only be used as a dipping sauce after it has been brought to a boil and allowed to boil for 5 minutes. This will destroy any salmonella bacteria introduced by the chicken.

Nutrients per Serving: Calories: 268, Calories from Fat: 23%, Total Fat: 7 g, Saturated Fat: 1 g, Protein: 26 g, Carbohydrate: 25 g, Cholesterol: 54 mg, Sodium: 516 mg, Fiber: 4 g, Iron: 3 mg, Calcium: 47 mg, Vitamin A: 393 RE, Vitamin C: 4 mg, Sugar: 6 g
Dietary Exchanges: 1 Vegetable, 1½ Starch, 2 Meat

Grilled Chicken, Rice & Veggies

Tex-Mex Flank Steak Salad

6 ounces beef flank steak
½ teaspoon Mexican seasoning blend or chili powder
⅛ teaspoon salt
Nonstick olive oil cooking spray

4 cups packaged mixed salad greens
1 can (11 ounces) mandarin orange sections, drained
2 tablespoons green taco sauce

1. Very thinly slice steak across the grain. Combine beef slices, Mexican seasoning and salt.

2. Lightly spray large nonstick skillet with cooking spray. Heat over medium-high heat. Add steak strips. Cook and stir 1 to 2 minutes or to desired doneness.

3. Toss together greens and orange sections. Arrange on serving plates. Top with warm steak. Drizzle with taco sauce.

Makes 2 servings

Tip: Flank steak is a lean cut of meat, which makes it an excellent choice for low-fat cooking. Cutting it across the grain into very thin strips helps to tenderize it.

Nutrients per Serving: Calories: 240, Calories from Fat: 25%, Total Fat: 7 g, Saturated Fat: 3 g, Protein: 25 g, Carbohydrate: 21 g, Cholesterol: 37 mg, Sodium: 388 mg, Fiber: 2 g, Iron: 3 mg, Calcium: 27 mg, Vitamin A: 137 RE, Vitamin C: 60 mg, Sugar: 3 g
Dietary Exchanges: 2 Vegetable, 1 Fruit, 2 Meat

Chicken & Wild Rice Skillet Dinner

1 teaspoon reduced-fat
   margarine
2 ounces boneless skinless
   chicken breast, cut into
   strips (about ½ chicken
   breast)

1 package (5 ounces)
   long-grain and wild rice
   mix with seasoning
½ cup water
3 dried apricots, cut up

1. Melt margarine in small skillet over medium-high heat. Add chicken; cook and stir 3 to 5 minutes or until no longer pink.

2. Meanwhile, measure ¼ cup of the rice and 1 tablespoon plus ½ teaspoon of the seasoning mix. Reserve remaining rice and seasoning mix for another use.

3. Add rice, seasoning mix, water and apricots to skillet; mix well. Bring to a boil. Cover and reduce heat to low; simmer 25 minutes or until liquid is absorbed and rice is tender. *Makes 1 serving*

Nutrients per Serving: Calories: 314, Calories from Fat: 13%, Total Fat: 5 g, Saturated Fat: 1 g, Protein: 24 g, Carbohydrate: 44 g, Cholesterol: 52 mg, Sodium: 669 mg, Fiber: 3 g, Iron: 1 mg, Calcium: 16 mg, Vitamin A: 155 RE, Vitamin C: <1 mg, Sugar: 6 g
Dietary Exchanges: 3 Starch, 2 Meat

Polenta with Fresh Tomato-Bean Salsa

½ (16-ounce) package
  prepared polenta
Nonstick cooking spray
1⅓ cups chopped plum
  tomatoes
⅔ cup canned black beans or
  red kidney beans, rinsed
  and drained

2 tablespoons chopped fresh
  basil leaves
¼ teaspoon black pepper
2 tablespoons grated
  Parmesan cheese

1. Preheat oven to 450°F. Cut polenta into ¼-inch-thick slices. Lightly spray shallow baking pan with cooking spray. Place polenta slices in a single layer in baking pan. Lightly spray top of polenta with cooking spray. Bake 15 to 20 minutes or until edges are slightly brown.

2. Meanwhile, stir together tomatoes, beans, basil and pepper. Let stand at room temperature 15 minutes to blend flavors.

3. Arrange polenta on serving plates. Spoon tomato mixture on top. Sprinkle with cheese.   *Makes 2 servings*

Recipe Tip: Salsa may be cooked, if desired. Cook and stir tomatoes and beans in large skillet over medium heat until hot. Stir in basil and pepper. Serve as directed.

Nutrients per Serving: Calories: 286, Calories from Fat: 17%, Total Fat: 6 g, Saturated Fat: 2 g, Protein: 14 g, Carbohydrate: 48 g, Cholesterol: 9 mg, Sodium: 548 mg, Fiber: 8 g, Iron: 4 mg, Calcium: 99 mg, Vitamin A: 220 RE, Vitamin C: 37 mg, Sugar: 10 g
Dietary Exchanges: 1 Vegetable, 3 Starch, 1 Fat

Polenta with Fresh Tomato-Bean Salsa

Warm Chutney Chicken Salad

Nonstick olive oil cooking spray
6 ounces boneless skinless chicken breasts, cut into bite-size pieces
⅓ cup mango chutney
¼ cup water

1 tablespoon Dijon mustard
4 cups packaged mixed salad greens
1 cup chopped peeled mango or papaya
Sliced green onions (optional)

1. Spray medium nonstick skillet with cooking spray. Heat over medium-high heat. Add chicken; cook and stir 2 to 3 minutes or until no longer pink. Stir in chutney, water and mustard. Cook and stir just until hot. Cool slightly.

2. Toss together salad greens and mango. Arrange on serving plates.

3. Spoon chicken mixture onto greens. Garnish with green onions, if desired.   *Makes 2 servings*

Tip: Mango chutney is a spicy, chunky condiment most often used as an accompaniment to Indian curries. It ranges in spiciness from fairly mild to hot.

Nutrients per Serving: Calories: 277, Calories from Fat: 10%, Total Fat: 3 g, Saturated Fat: 1 g, Protein: 21 g, Carbohydrate: 42 g, Cholesterol: 52 mg, Sodium: 117 mg, Fiber: 4 g, Iron: 1 mg, Calcium: 33 mg, Vitamin A: 427 RE, Vitamin C: 30 mg, Sugar: 37 g
Dietary Exchanges: 2 Vegetable, 2 Fruit, 2 Meat

Warm Chutney Chicken Salad

Fabulous
FLAVORS

Jerk Turkey Salad

6 ounces turkey breast
tenderloin

1½ teaspoons Caribbean jerk
seasoning

4 cups packaged mixed
salad greens

¾ cup sliced peeled
cucumber

⅔ cup chopped fresh
pineapple

⅔ cup quartered strawberries
or raspberries

½ cup slivered peeled jicama
or sliced celery

1 green onion, sliced

¼ cup lime juice

3 tablespoons honey

1. Prepare grill for direct grilling. Rub turkey with jerk seasoning.

2. Grill turkey over medium coals 15 to 20 minutes or until turkey is no longer pink and juices run clear, turning once. Remove from grill and cool.

3. Cut turkey into bite-size pieces. Toss together greens, turkey, cucumber, pineapple, strawberries, jicama and green onion.

4. Combine lime juice and honey. Toss with greens mixture. Serve immediately. *Makes 2 servings*

Nutrients per Serving: Calories: 265, Calories from Fat: 6%, Total Fat: 2 g, Saturated Fat: 1 g, Protein: 17 g, Carbohydrate: 48 g, Cholesterol: 34 mg, Sodium: 356 mg, Fiber: 6 g, Iron: 2 mg, Calcium: 37 mg, Vitamin A: 13 RE, Vitamin C: 56 mg, Sugar: 39 g
Dietary Exchanges: 2 Vegetable, 2 Fruit, 2 Meat

Jerk Turkey Salad

Jamaican Jerk Turkey Wraps

6 ounces turkey breast tenderloin

1½ teaspoons Caribbean jerk seasoning

4 cups broccoli slaw

1 large tomato, seeded and chopped (about 1⅓ cups)

⅓ cup reduced-fat cole slaw dressing

2 jalapeño peppers,* finely chopped

2 tablespoons mustard (optional)

8 (8-inch) fat-free flour tortillas, warmed

*Jalapeño peppers can sting and irritate the skin; wear rubber gloves when handling peppers and do not touch eyes. Wash hands after handling peppers.

1. Prepare grill for direct grilling. Rub jerk seasoning on both sides of turkey.

2. Grill turkey over medium coals 15 to 20 minutes or until turkey is no longer pink and juices run clear, turning once. Thinly slice turkey.

3. Toss together broccoli slaw, tomato, dressing, jalapeño pepper and mustard. Place sliced turkey on tortillas; spoon broccoli slaw mixture on top. Wrap to enclose. Serve immediately.

Makes 4 servings

Tip: Broccoli slaw, which is slivered broccoli stalks, is now available in most supermarkets. Add it to wraps or pita bread sandwiches, or toss it with coleslaw dressing for a nutritious salad.

Nutrients per Serving: Calories: 356, Calories from Fat: 30%, Total Fat: 12 g, Saturated Fat: 2 g, Protein: 20 g, Carbohydrate: 40 g, Cholesterol: 41 mg, Sodium: 1058 mg, Fiber: 15 g, Iron: 1 mg, Calcium: 62 mg, Vitamin A: 59 RE, Vitamin C: 15 mg, Sugar: 5 g
Dietary Exchanges: 2 Vegetable, 2 Starch, 2 Meat, 1 Fat

Jamaican Jerk Turkey Wraps

Thai Curry Stir-Fry

½ cup fat-free, reduced-sodium chicken broth

2 teaspoons cornstarch

1½ teaspoons curry powder

2 teaspoons reduced-sodium soy sauce

⅛ teaspoon crushed red pepper

Nonstick olive oil cooking spray

3 green onions, sliced

2 cloves garlic, minced

2 cups broccoli florets

⅔ cup sliced carrot

1½ teaspoons olive oil

6 ounces boneless skinless chicken breast, cut into bite-size pieces

⅔ cup hot cooked rice, prepared without salt

1. Stir together broth, cornstarch, curry powder, soy sauce and red pepper. Set aside.

2. Spray nonstick wok or large nonstick skillet with cooking spray. Heat over medium-high heat. Add onions and garlic; stir-fry 1 minute. Remove from wok.

3. Add broccoli and carrot to wok; stir-fry 2 to 3 minutes or until crisp-tender. Remove from wok.

4. Add oil to hot wok. Add chicken and stir-fry 2 to 3 minutes or until no longer pink. Stir broth mixture. Add to wok. Cook and stir until broth mixture comes to a boil and thickens slightly. Return all vegetables to wok. Heat through.

5. Serve remaining chicken mixture with rice.

Makes 2 servings

Nutrients per Serving: Calories: 273, Calories from Fat: 20%, Total Fat: 6 g, Saturated Fat: 1 g, Protein: 28 g, Carbohydrate: 27 g, Cholesterol: 57 mg, Sodium: 308 mg, Fiber: 5 g, Iron: 3 mg, Calcium: 88 mg, Vitamin A: 1181 RE, Vitamin C: 88 mg, Sugar: 5 g
Dietary Exchanges: 2 Vegetable, 1 Starch, 3 Meat

Thai Curry Stir-Fry

Curried Chicken & Pasta Salad

¼ cup fat-free, reduced sodium chicken broth
1 teaspoon cornstarch
½ teaspoon curry powder
1 teaspoon reduced-sodium soy sauce
⅛ teaspoon crushed red pepper
Nonstick cooking spray
1 green onion, sliced
1 clove garlic, minced
1 cup broccoli florets
⅓ cup carrot slices
1 teaspoon olive oil
4 ounces boneless skinless chicken breast, cut into bite-size pieces
⅔ cup cooked small shell pasta
½ cup sliced celery
⅓ cup dried cranberries or tart cherries
¼ cup fat-free honey Dijon salad dressing
Salt
2 lettuce leaves

1. Stir together broth, cornstarch, curry powder, soy sauce and red pepper. Set aside.

2. Spray nonstick wok or medium nonstick skillet with cooking spray. Heat over medium-high heat. Add onion and garlic; stir-fry 1 minute. Remove from wok to bowl.

3. Add broccoli and carrots to wok; stir-fry 2 to 3 minutes or until crisp-tender. Remove from wok to bowl.

4. Add oil to wok; add chicken and stir-fry 2 to 3 minutes or until no longer pink. Stir broth mixture. Add to wok. Cook and stir until sauce comes to a boil and thickens slightly. Add to vegetable mixture. Cool 15 minutes.

5. Toss chicken mixture, pasta, celery, cranberries and salad dressing. Season to taste with salt. Cover and refrigerate 1 to 24 hours. Serve on lettuce leaves.   *Makes 2 servings*

Nutrients per Serving: Calories: 322, Calories from Fat: 11%, Total Fat: 4 g, Saturated Fat: 1 g, Protein: 18 g, Carbohydrate: 55 g, Cholesterol: 29 mg, Sodium: 517 mg, Fiber: 5 g, Iron: 3 mg, Calcium: 89 mg, Vitamin A: 818 RE, Vitamin C: 64 mg, Sugar: 9 g
Dietary Exchanges: 2 Vegetable, 3 Starch, 1 Meat

Pork, Mushrooms, Onion & Pepper

½ pound boneless thin-cut
    pork loin chops
Salt
Garlic pepper
Nonstick cooking spray
1 teaspoon olive oil
1½ cups thinly sliced
    mushrooms

1 cup diced onion
1 cup diced red bell pepper
1 clove garlic, minced
⅛ teaspoon salt
¼ cup red wine

1. Sprinkle both sides of pork chops lightly with salt and garlic pepper. Coat large nonstick skillet with cooking spray; heat over medium-low heat. Cook pork 1 to 2 minutes per side side or until brown and barely pink in center. Remove from skillet; keep warm.

2. Heat oil over medium heat in same nonstick skillet. Add mushrooms, onion, bell pepper, garlic and salt. Cook 8 to 10 minutes or until vegetables are soft. Add wine, a little at a time, stirring to remove any browned bits from bottom of skillet. Bring to a boil; boil 1 minute. Serve vegetable mixture over pork chops.

Makes 2 servings

Tip: Wine adds a lot of flavor to recipes. Just be sure that wine mixtures cook for 2 or 3 minutes to burn off the alcohol and allow the flavors to blend.

Nutrients per Serving: Calories: 298, Calories from Fat: 40%, Total Fat: 13 g, Saturated Fat: 4 g, Protein: 27 g, Carbohydrate: 13 g, Cholesterol: 54 mg, Sodium: 206 mg, Fiber: 3 g, Iron: 3 mg, Calcium: 55 mg, Vitamin A: 25 RE, Vitamin C: 41 mg, Sugar: 4 g
Dietary Exchanges: 3 Vegetable, 3 Meat, 1 Fat

Pork & Vegetable Wraps

½ pound boneless thin-cut
    pork loin chops
Salt
Garlic pepper
Nonstick cooking spray
1 tablespoon reduced-fat
    mayonnaise
2 teaspoons Dijon mustard

4 (8-inch) fat-free flour
    tortillas
1 cup torn spinach leaves
½ peeled cucumber, diced
1 medium tomato, chopped
Black pepper
Celery salt (optional)

1. Sprinkle both sides of pork lighly with salt and garlic pepper. Coat large nonstick skillet with cooking spray; heat over medium-low heat. Cook pork 1 to 2 minutes per side or until brown and barely pink in center. Remove from skillet and cool.

2. Cut pork into thin strips.

3. Combine mayonnaise and mustard in small cup. Spread on one side of each tortilla. Top with pork, spinach, cucumber and tomato. Season to taste with pepper and celery salt, if desired.

4. Fold in sides of tortilla and roll up to enclose filling. Lay seam side down and cut in half. Serve immediately. *Makes 2 servings*

Tip: To reduce carbohydrate, omit the tortillas and serve as a salad with your favorite reduced-fat dressing.

Nutrients per Serving: Calories: 327, Calories from Fat: 30%, Total Fat: 11 g, Saturated Fat: 3 g, Protein: 24 g, Carbohydrate: 33 g, Cholesterol: 40 mg, Sodium: 637 mg, Fiber: 14 g, Iron: 3 mg, Calcium: 104 mg, Vitamin A: 244 RE, Vitamin C: 24 mg, Sugar: 4 g
Dietary Exchanges: 3 Vegetable, 1 Starch, 3 Meat, ½ Fat

Pork & Vegetable Wrap

Southwest Roasted Salmon & Corn

2 ears fresh corn, unhusked

1 (6-ounce) salmon fillet, cut into 2 equal pieces

1 tablespoon plus 1 teaspoon fresh lime juice, divided

1 clove garlic, minced

½ teaspoon chili powder

¼ teaspoon ground cumin

¼ teaspoon oregano leaves

⅛ teaspoon salt, divided

⅛ teaspoon black pepper

2 teaspoons margarine, melted

2 teaspoons minced fresh cilantro

1. Preheat oven to 400°F. Spray shallow 1-quart baking dish with nonstick cooking spray. Pull back husks from each ear of corn, leaving husks attached. Discard silk. Soak corn in cold water 20 minutes.

2. Place salmon, skin side down, in prepared dish. Pour 1 tablespoon lime juice over fillets. Marinate at room temperature 15 minutes.

3. Combine garlic, chili powder, cumin, oregano, half of salt and pepper in small bowl. Pat salmon lightly with paper towel. Rub garlic mixture on tops and sides of salmon.

4. Remove corn from water; pat kernels dry with paper towels. Bring husks back up over each ear; secure at top with thin strips of corn husk. Place corn on one side of oven rack. Roast 10 minutes; turn.

5. Place salmon in baking dish on other side of oven rack. Roast 15 minutes or until salmon is opaque and flakes when tested with fork, and corn is tender.

6. Combine margarine, cilantro, remaining 1 teaspoon lime juice and remaining salt in small bowl. Remove husks from corn. Brush over corn. Serve corn with salmon. *Makes 2 servings*

Nutrients per Serving: Calories: 186, Calories from Fat: 29%, Total Fat: 6 g, Saturated Fat: 1 g, Protein: 19 g, Carbohydrate: 16 g, Cholesterol: 43 mg, Sodium: 243 mg, Fiber: 2 g, Iron: 1 mg, Calcium: 24 mg, Vitamin A: 94 RE, Vitamin C: 6 mg, Sugar: 1 g
Dietary Exchanges: 1 Starch, 1 Meat

Southwest Roasted Salmon & Corn

Salmon, Corn & Barley Chowder

1 teaspoon canola oil
¼ cup chopped onion
1 clove garlic, minced
2½ cups fat-free reduced-sodium chicken broth
¼ cup quick-cooking barley
1 tablespoon water
1 tablespoon all-purpose flour
1 can (4 ounces) salmon, drained

1 cup frozen corn, thawed
⅓ cup reduced-fat (2%) milk
½ teaspoon chili powder
¼ teaspoon ground cumin
¼ teaspoon dried oregano leaves
⅛ teaspoon salt
1 tablespoon minced cilantro
⅛ teaspoon black pepper
Lime wedges (optional)

1. Heat oil in medium saucepan over medium heat until hot. Add onion and garlic. Cook and stir 1 to 2 minutes or until onion is tender.

2. Add broth and bring to a boil. Stir in barley. Cover; reduce heat to low. Simmer 10 minutes or until barley is tender.

3. Stir water slowly into flour in cup until smooth. Remove and discard bones and skin from salmon; flake salmon into bite size pieces.

4. Add corn, salmon and milk to saucepan, stirring to blend. Stir in flour mixture, then chili powder, cumin, oregano and salt. Simmer gently 2 to 3 minutes or until slightly thickened. Stir in cilantro and pepper. Serve with lime wedges. *Makes 2 (2¼ cups) servings*

Tip: Cilantro is a fresh leafy herb that has a distinctive flavor and aroma. Its flavor complements spicy foods, especially Mexican, Caribbean, Thai and Vietnamese dishes.

Nutrients per Serving: Calories: 321, Calories from Fat: 20%, Total Fat: 7 g, Saturated Fat: 1 g, Protein: 26 g, Carbohydrate: 40 g, Cholesterol: 46 mg, Sodium: 310 mg, Fiber: 27g, Iron: 1 mg, Calcium: 24 mg, Vitamin A: 94 RE, Vitamin C: 6 mg, Sugar: 1 g
Dietary Exchanges: 3 Starch, 2 Lean Meat

Salmon, Corn & Barley Chowder

Turkey Tenderloin with Caramelized Vegetables

1 cup diced green bell
　peppers
1 cup thinly sliced carrots
1 cup thin onion wedges
8 ounces mushrooms, cut
　into halves*
2 cloves garlic, chopped
1 tablespoon balsamic
　vinegar or red wine
　vinegar

1 teaspoon olive oil
$\frac{1}{8}$ teaspoon salt, divided
$\frac{1}{8}$ teaspoon black pepper,
　divided
1$\frac{1}{2}$ teaspoons country-style
　Dijon mustard
6 ounces turkey tenderloin
$\frac{1}{2}$ teaspoon paprika
　Nonstick cooking spray

*Cut large mushrooms into quarters.

1. Preheat oven to 400°F. Line 15×10-inch baking pan with heavy-duty foil.

2. Combine bell peppers, carrots, onions, mushrooms, garlic, vinegar, oil, half of salt and half of pepper in large bowl, tossing to coat vegetables evenly with seasonings. Spread vegetables onto prepared pan. Bake 15 minutes.

3. Meanwhile, spread mustard over top of turkey. Combine paprika, remaining salt and pepper in small bowl. Sprinkle over turkey. Lightly spray top of turkey with cooking spray.

4. Remove vegetables from oven. Stir vegetables and push to edges of pan. Place turkey in center of vegetables.

5. Roast 20 minutes. Stir vegetables. Roast 20 minutes more or until turkey is no longer pink in center (170°F). Let turkey stand 5 minutes. Carve turkey across the grain into $\frac{1}{2}$-inch-thick slices.

6. Divide sliced turkey between two plates. Place 1 cup vegetables on each plate. *Makes 2 servings*

Nutrients per Serving: Calories: 232, Calories from Fat: 18%, Total Fat: 5 g, Saturated Fat: 1 g, Protein: 20 g, Carbohydrate: 30 g, Cholesterol: 34 mg, Sodium: 215 mg, Fiber: 7 g, Iron: 3 mg, Calcium: 66 mg, Vitamin A: 1634 RE, Vitamin C: 116 mg, Sugar: 14 g
Dietary Exchanges: 4 Vegetable, 2 Meat

Turkey Paprikash

1 cup yolk-free extra-broad
noodles
Nonstick cooking spray
6 ounces turkey tenderloin,
cut into ½-inch pieces
8 ounces mushrooms, sliced
1 cup diced green bell
pepper
1 cup thinly sliced carrots
1 cup slivered onion
2 cloves garlic, minced

2 teaspoons paprika
¾ cup water
1 tablespoon plus
1½ teaspoons tomato
paste
⅛ teaspoon salt
⅛ teaspoon black pepper
3 tablespoons reduced-fat
sour cream
2 teaspoons minced fresh
parsley

1. Cook noodles according to package directions, omitting salt.
Drain and keep warm.

2. Meanwhile, spray medium skillet with cooking spray. Heat over
medium heat until hot. Add turkey; cook and stir 1 minute or until
browned on all sides. Add mushrooms, bell pepper, carrots and
onion; cook and stir 3 minutes or until crisp-tender. Add garlic and
paprika. Cook and stir 30 seconds or until garlic is fragrant.

3. Stir in water, tomato paste, salt and pepper. Simmer, uncovered,
10 minutes. Remove from heat; stir in noodles. Stir several
tablespoons of liquid into sour cream, then stir sour cream mixture
into turkey mixture. Top each serving with parsley.

Makes 2 servings

Tip: For added flavor in this recipe, add tomato paste to the skillet
after cooking garlic. Cook tomato paste for 2 or 3 minutes before
adding water and seasonings, then proceed with the recipe as
directed.

Nutrients per Serving: Calories: 330, Calories from Fat: 19%, Total Fat: 7 g,
Saturated Fat: 3 g, Protein: 26 g, Carbohydrate: 43 g, Cholesterol: 47 mg,
Sodium: 484 mg, Fiber: 8 g, Iron: 4 mg, Calcium: 112 mg, Vitamin A: 1796 RE,
Vitamin C: 125 mg, Sugar: 16 g
Dietary Exchanges: 3 Vegetable, 2 Starch, 2 Meat

Meatless DINNERS

Grilled Mozzarella & Roasted Red Pepper Sandwich

1 tablespoon reduced-fat
   olive oil vinaigrette or
   Italian salad dressing
2 slices (2 ounces) Italian-
   style sandwich bread
⅓ cup roasted red peppers,
   rinsed, drained and
   patted dry

Basil leaves (optional)
2 slices (1 ounce each) part-
   skim mozzarella or
   reduced-fat Swiss cheese
Nonstick olive oil cooking
   spray

1. Brush dressing on one side of one slice of bread; top with peppers, basil, if desired, cheese and second bread slice. Lightly spray both sides of sandwich with cooking spray.

2. Heat skillet over medium heat until hot. Place sandwich in skillet and grill 4 to 5 minutes on each side until brown and cheese is melted. *Makes 1 serving*

Nutrients per Serving: Calories: 303, Calories from Fat: 29%, Total Fat: 9 g, Saturated Fat: 5 g, Protein: 16 g, Carbohydrate: 35 g, Cholesterol: 25 mg, Sodium: 727 mg, Fiber: 2 g, Iron: 3 mg, Calcium: 324 mg, Vitamin A: 495 RE, Vitamin C: 43 mg, Sugar: 6 g
Dietary Exchanges: 1 Vegetable, 2 Starch, 1 Meat, 1½ Fat

Grilled Mozzarella & Roasted Red Pepper Sandwich

Spaghetti Squash Primavera

1 teaspoon olive oil
¼ cup diced green bell
  pepper
¼ cup diced zucchini
¼ cup sliced mushrooms
¼ cup diced carrot
¼ cup sliced green onions
2 cloves garlic, minced
1 plum tomato, diced
1 tablespoon red wine or
  water

½ teaspoon dried basil
  leaves
¼ teaspoon salt
⅛ teaspoon black pepper
2 cups cooked spaghetti
  squash
2 tablespoons grated
  Parmesan cheese

1. Heat oil in medium skillet over low heat. Add bell pepper,
zucchini, mushrooms, carrot, green onions and garlic; cook 10 to
12 minutes or until crisp-tender, stirring ocassionally. Stir in tomato,
wine, basil, salt and black pepper; cook 4 to 5 minutes, stirring once
or twice.

2. Serve vegetables over spaghetti squash. Top with cheese.

Makes 2 servings

Tip: To cook spaghetti squash, cut the squash in half lengthwise.
Remove and discard seeds. Place squash, cut side down, in a 13×9-
inch baking dish sprayed with nonstick cooking spray. Bake at 350°F
for 45 minutes to 1 hour or until tender. Using a fork, remove
spaghetti-like strands from hot squash.

Nutrients per Serving: Calories: 116, Calories from Fat: 39%, Total Fat: 5 g,
Saturated Fat: 1 g, Protein: 5 g, Carbohydrate: 15 g, Cholesterol: 4 mg,
Sodium: 396 mg, Fiber: 5 g, Iron: 2 mg, Calcium: 154 mg, Vitamin A: 497 RE,
Vitamin C: 46 mg, Sugar: 7 g
Dietary Exchanges: 3 Vegetable, 1 Fat

Spaghetti Squash Primavera

Vegetable & Tofu Gratin

Nonstick cooking spray
1 teaspoon olive oil
¾ cup thinly sliced fennel bulb
¾ cup thinly sliced onion
2 cloves garlic, minced
¾ cup cooked brown rice
2 tablespoons balsamic or red wine vinegar, divided
2 teaspoons dried Italian seasoning, divided

3 ounces firm tofu, crumbled
¼ cup crumbled feta cheese
6 ounces ripe plum tomatoes, sliced ¼ inch thick
6 ounces zucchini, sliced ¼ inch thick
⅛ teaspoon salt
⅛ teaspoon black pepper
¼ cup fresh bread crumbs
2 tablespoons grated fresh Parmesan cheese

1. Preheat oven to 400°F. Spray 1-quart shallow baking dish with nonstick cooking spray.

2. Spray medium skillet with cooking spray. Heat oil in skillet over medium heat until hot. Add fennel and onion. Cook 10 minutes or until tender and lightly browned, stirring frequently. Add garlic; cook and stir 1 minute. Spread over bottom of prepared baking dish.

3. Combine rice, 1 tablespoon vinegar and ½ teaspoon Italian seasoning in small bowl. Spread over onion mixture.

4. Combine tofu, feta cheese, remaining 1 tablespoon vinegar and 1 teaspoon Italian seasoning in small bowl; mix. Spoon over rice. Top with alternating rows of tomato and zucchini slices. Sprinkle with salt and pepper.

6. Combine bread crumbs, Parmesan cheese and remaining ½ teaspoon Italian seasoning in small bowl. Sprinkle over top. Spray bread crumb topping lightly with nonstick cooking spray. Bake 30 minutes or until heated through and topping is browned.

Makes 2 servings

Nutrients per Serving: Calories: 336, Calories from Fat: 31%, Total Fat: 12 g, Saturated Fat: 4 g, Protein: 16 g, Carbohydrate: 44 g, Cholesterol: 16 mg, Sodium: 473 mg, Fiber: 7 g, Iron: 7 mg, Calcium: 293 mg, Vitamin A: 120 RE, Vitamin C: 34 mg, Sugar: 11 g
Dietary Exchanges: 3 Vegetable, 2 Starch, 1 Meat, 1½ Fat

Vegetable & Tofu Gratin

Curried Eggplant, Squash & Chick-Pea Stew

1 teaspoon olive oil
½ cup diced red bell pepper
¼ cup diced onion
1¼ teaspoons curry powder
1 clove garlic, minced
½ teaspoon salt
1¼ cups peeled, cubed eggplant
¾ cup peeled, cubed acorn or butternut squash

⅔ cup rinsed and drained canned chick-peas
½ cup vegetable broth or water
3 tablespoons white wine
Hot pepper sauce (optional)
¼ cup lemon-flavored sugar-free yogurt
2 tablespoons chopped fresh parsley

1. Heat oil in medium saucepan over medium heat. Add bell pepper and onion; cook and stir 5 minutes. Stir in curry powder, garlic and salt. Add eggplant, squash, chick-peas, broth and wine to saucepan. Cover; bring to a boil. Reduce heat and simmer 20 to 25 minutes just until squash and eggplant are tender.

2. Season to taste with pepper sauce, if desired. Serve with yogurt and parsley.   *Makes 2 servings*

Nutrients per Serving: Calories: 216, Calories from Fat: 14%, Total Fat: 4 g, Saturated Fat: <1 g, Protein: 7 g, Carbohydrate: 38 g, Cholesterol: 0 mg, Sodium: 477 mg, Fiber: 10 g, Iron: 2 mg, Calcium: 110 mg, Vitamin A: 199 RE, Vitamin C: 63 mg
Dietary Exchanges: 2½ Starch, 1 Fat

French Bread Portobello Pizza

Nonstick cooking spray
⅓ cup sliced portobello
    mushroom cap
1 clove garlic, minced
½ cup chopped tomato
1 tablespoon tomato sauce
1 (2-ounce) piece French
    bread, cut in half
    lengthwise

¼ cup (1 ounce) shredded
    reduced-fat Italian chese
    blend or part-skim
    mozzarella cheese
Red pepper flakes
    (optional)

1. Preheat oven to 450°F. Spray small skillet with cooking spray. Heat over medium-low heat until hot. Cook and stir mushrooms and garlic 5 to 7 minutes or until mushrooms are slightly soft.

2. Stir in tomato and tomato sauce; cook 5 minutes. Spread mixture over cut sides of bread. Sprinkle with cheese. Bake 15 minutes until cheese is melted. Sprinkle with pepper flakes, if desired.

Makes 1 serving

Tip: Portobello mushrooms have very large dark brown caps and thick, tough stems. Because they have a firm texture when cooked, they are sometimes substituted for beef in vegetarian dishes. Baby portobello mushrooms, which are available in some produce markets, are a good choice for this recipe.

Nutrients per Serving: Calories: 246, Calories from Fat: 13%, Total Fat: 4 g, Saturated Fat: 1 g, Protein: 15 g, Carbohydrate: 39 g, Cholesterol: 4 mg, Sodium: 661 mg, Fiber: 4 g, Iron: 2 mg, Calcium: 67 mg, Vitamin A: 84 RE, Vitamin C: 24 mg, Sugar: 6 g
Dietary Exchanges: 2 Vegetable, 2 Starch, 1 Meat

Red Bean & Corn Salad with Lime-Cumin Dressing

2 tablespoons fresh lime juice

1½ teaspoons canola oil

½ teaspoon ground cumin

½ teaspoon water

⅛ teaspoon salt

¾ cup canned red beans, rinsed and drained

½ cup frozen corn with bell pepper and onion, thawed

¼ cup chopped tomato

2 tablespoons chopped green onion, divided

2 large romaine lettuce leaves

1. Whisk together lime juice, oil, cumin, water and salt in medium bowl.

2. Add beans, corn, tomato and 1 tablespoon green onion; toss to coat. Serve on lettuce leaves. Top with remaining green onion.

Makes 1 serving

Nutrients per Serving: Calories: 198, Calories from Fat: 18%, Total Fat: 4 g, Saturated Fat: <1 g, Protein: 8 g, Carbohydrate: 33 g, Cholesterol: 0 mg, Sodium: 908 mg, Fiber: 9 g, Iron: 2 mg, Calcium: 40 mg, Vitamin A: 71 RE, Vitamin C: 16 mg, Sugar: 7 g
Dietary Exchanges: 2 Starch, 1 Meat

Red Bean & Corn Salad with Lime-Cumin Dressing

Cheesy Baked Barley

2 cups water
½ cup medium pearled
  barley
½ teaspoon salt, divided
  Nonstick cooking spray
½ cup diced onion
½ cup diced zucchini
½ cup diced red bell pepper

1½ teaspoons all-purpose
  flour
  Seasoned pepper
¾ cup fat-free (skim) milk
1 cup (4 ounces) shredded
  reduced-fat Italian blend
  cheese, divided
1 tablespoon Dijon mustard

1. Bring water to a boil in 1-quart saucepan. Add barley and
¼ teaspoon salt. Cover; reduce heat and simmer 45 minutes or until
barley is tender and most water is evaporated. Let stand covered,
5 minutes.

2. Preheat oven to 375°F. Spray medium skillet with cooking spray.
Cook onion, zucchini and bell pepper over medium-low heat about
10 minutes or until soft. Stir in flour, remaining ¼ teaspoon salt and
seasoned pepper to taste; cook 1 to 2 minutes. Add milk, stirring
constantly; cook and stir until slightly thickened. Remove from heat
and add barley, ¾ cup cheese and mustard; stir until cheese is
melted.

3. Spread in even layer in casserole. Sprinkle with remaining ¼ cup
cheese. Bake 20 minutes or until hot. Preheat broiler. Broil casserole
1 to 2 minutes or until cheese is lightly browned.

Makes 2 servings

Tip: Barley is an excellent substitute for rice. When cooked, it has a
slightly chewy texture and mild nutty flavor. Not only does it have
four times the fiber of white rice, but barley also contains 20
percent less carbohydrate than white rice.

Nutrients per Serving: Calories: 362, Calories from Fat: 23%, Total Fat: 9 g,
Saturated Fat: 4 g, Protein: 20 g, Carbohydrate: 50 g, Cholesterol: 32 mg,
Sodium: 1159 mg, Fiber: 6 g, Iron: 2 mg, Calcium: 555 mg, Vitamin A: 257 RE,
Vitamin C: 12 mg, Sugar: 7 g
Dietary Exchanges: 2 Vegetable, 2½ Starch, 2 Meat, ½ Fat

Cheesy Baked Barley

Orange Ginger Tofu & Noodles

⅔ cup orange juice

3 tablespoons reduced-sodium soy sauce

½ to 1 teaspoon minced ginger

1 clove garlic, minced

¼ teaspoon red pepper flakes

5 ounces extra-firm tofu, well drained and cut into ½-inch cubes

1½ teaspoons cornstarch

1 teaspoon canola or peanut oil

2 cups fresh cut-up vegetables, such as broccoli, carrots, onion and snow peas

1½ cups hot cooked vermicelli

1. Combine orange juice, soy sauce, ginger, garlic and red pepper in resealable plastic food storage bag; add tofu. Marinate 20 to 30 minutes. Drain tofu, reserving marinade. Stir marinade into cornstarch until smooth.

2. Heat oil in large nonstick skillet or wok over medium-high heat. Add vegetables; stir-fry 2 to 3 minutes or until vegetables are crisp-tender. add tofu; stir-fry 1 minute. Stir reserved marinade mixture; add to skillet. Bring to a boil; boil 1 minute. Serve over vermicelli.

Makes 2 servings

Tip: To drain tofu, place it in a colander and let it stand 5 minutes, then place it on several layers of paper towels. If extra-firm tofu is not available, use firm tofu; drain as directed above, cover with paper towels and place a small heavy plate on top. Let stand for 5 or 10 minutes, then cut into cubes.

Nutrients per Serving: Calories: 305, Calories from Fat: 20%, Total Fat: 7 g, Saturated Fat: 1 g, Protein: 19 g, Carbohydrate: 42 g, Cholesterol: 0 mg, Sodium: 824 mg, Fiber: 6 g, Iron: 8 mg, Calcium: 189 mg, Vitamin A: 91 RE, Vitamin C: 58 mg, Sugar: 14 g
Dietary Exchanges: 2 Vegetable, 2 Starch, 1 Meat, 1 Fat

Orange Ginger Tofu & Noodles

Delicious
DESSERTS

Baked Pear Dessert

2 tablespoons dried
  cranberries or raisins
1 tablespoon toasted sliced
  almonds
⅛ teaspoon cinnamon
⅓ cup unsweetened apple
  cider or apple juice,
  divided

1 medium (6-ounce)
  unpeeled pear, cut in
  half lengthwise and
  cored
½ cup vanilla sugar-free
  low-fat frozen ice cream
  or frozen yogurt

1. Preheat oven to 350°F. Combine cranberries, almonds, cinnamon and 1 teaspoon cider in small bowl.

2. Place pear halves, cut side up, in small baking dish. Mound almond mixture on top of pear halves. Pour remaining cider into dish. Cover with foil.

3. Bake pear halves 35 to 40 minutes or until pears are soft, spooning cider in dish over pears once or twice during baking. Serve warm and top with ice cream.   *Makes 2 servings*

Nutrients per Serving: Calories: 87, Calories from Fat: 19%, Total Fat: 2 g, Saturated Fat: <1 g, Protein: 1 g, Carbohydrate: 16 g, Cholesterol: 3 mg, Sodium: 13 mg, Fiber: 1 g, Iron: <1 mg, Calcium: 28 mg, Vitamin A: 11 RE, Vitamin C: 2 mg, Sugar: 11 g
Dietary Exchanges: 1 Fruit, ½ Fat

Baked Pear Dessert

Lemon Yogurt Pudding with Blueberry Sauce

1 cup plain nonfat yogurt
Grated peel of ½ lemon
1 tablespoon fresh lemon
   juice, divided
½ teaspoon vanilla
4 packets sugar substitute *or*
   equivalent of
   6 tablespoons sugar,
   divided

¾ cup fresh blueberries,
   divided
1½ teaspoon sugar
1 teaspoon cornstarch

1. Line strainer with cheesecloth or coffee filter and place over bowl. Spoon yogurt into lined strainer. Cover with plastic wrap and refrigerate 12 hours or overnight.

2. Discard drained liquid. Whisk together thickened yogurt, lemon peel, 1 tablespoon lemon juice, vanilla and 6 packets sugar substitute in large bowl until smooth. Cover and refrigerate 1 hour.

3. To prepare blueberry sauce, mash half the blueberries with fork. Combine mashed and whole blueberries, remaining 1 tablespoon lemon juice, sugar and cornstarch in small saucepan; mix well. Cook over medium-high heat about 4 minutes or until mixture has thickened. Remove from heat and cool 2 minutes. Stir in remaining 2 packets sugar substitute.

4. Divide yogurt mixture among 4 small dessert bowls or stemmed glasses. Top with warm blueberry sauce. Serve immediately.

Makes 2 servings

Nutrients per Serving: Calories: 124, Calories from Fat: 3%, Total Fat: <1 g, Saturated Fat: <1 g, Protein: 9 g, Carbohydrate: 22 g, Cholesterol: 2 mg, Sodium: 91 mg, Fiber: 2 g, Calcium: 145 mg, Vitamin A: 95 RE , Vitamin C: 22 mg, Sugar: 13 g
Dietary Exchanges: 1 Fruit, ½ Milk

Grilled Banana Splits

1 large ripe firm banana
½ teaspoon melted butter
2 tablespoons reduced-sugar, reduced calorie fat-free chocolate syrup
½ teaspoon orange liqueur (optional)

⅔ cup sugar-free vanilla ice cream
2 tablespoons toasted sliced almonds

1. Prepare grill for direct cooking

2. Cut unpeeled bananas lengthwise; brush melted butter over cut sides. Grill bananas, cut side down, over medium-hot coals 2 minutes or until lightly browned; turn. Grill 2 minutes or until tender.

3. Combine syrup and liqueur, if desired, in small bowl.

4. Cut bananas in half crosswise; carefully remove peel. Place 2 pieces banana in each bowl; top with ⅓ cup ice cream, 1 tablespoon chocolate syrup, and 1 tablespoon nuts; serve immediately.   *Makes 2 servings*

Nutrients per Serving: Calories: 198, Calories from Fat: 22%, Total Fat: 5 g, Saturated Fat: 1 g, Protein: 5 g, Carbohydrate: 33 g, Cholesterol: 3 mg, Sodium: 59 mg, Fiber: 2 g, Calcium: 60 mg, Vitamin A: 41 RE , Vitamin C: 5 mg, Sugar: 17 g
Dietary Exchanges: 1½ Fruit, 1 Starch, 1 Fat

Peaches & Cream Gingersnap Cups

1½ tablespoons gingersnap
   crumbs (2 snaps)
¼ teaspoon ground ginger
2 ounces reduced-fat cream
   cheese, softened
1 container (6 ounces) peach
   sugar-free, nonfat
   yogurt

¼ teaspoon vanilla
⅓ cup chopped fresh peach
   or drained canned
   peach slices in juice

1. Combine gingersnap crumbs and ginger in small bowl; set aside.

2. Beat cream cheese in small bowl at medium speed of electric mixer until smooth. Add yogurt and vanilla. Beat at low speed until smooth and well blended. Stir in chopped peach.

3. Divide peach mixture between two 6-ounce custard cups. Cover and refrigerate 1 hour. Top each serving with half of gingersnap crumb mixture just before serving.   *Makes 2 servings*

Note:: Instead of crushing the gingersnaps, serve them whole with the peaches & cream cups.

Nutrients per Serving: Calories: 148, Calories from Fat: 34%, Total Fat: 5 g, Saturated Fat: 3 g, Protein: 6 g, Carbohydrate: 18 g, Cholesterol: 16 mg, Sodium: 204 mg, Fiber: 1 g, Iron: <1 mg, Calcium: 37 mg, Vitamin A: 122 RE, Vitamin C: 2 mg, Sugar: 10 g
Dietary Exchanges: 1 Starch, 1 Fat, ½ Milk

Peaches & Cream Gingersnap Cups

Cinnamon Tortilla with Cream Cheese & Strawberries

1 packet sugar substitute or
  equivalent of
  2 teaspoons sugar
⅛ teaspoon ground
  cinnamon
1 (6-inch) fat-free flour
  tortilla

Nonstick cooking spray
1 tablespoon reduced-fat
  soft cream cheese
⅓ cup fresh strawberry slices

1. Combine sugar substitute and cinnamon in cup; mix well. Heat large nonstick skillet over medium heat.

2. Lightly spray one side of tortilla with cooking spray; sprinkle with cinnamon mixture.

3. Place tortilla, cinnamon side down, in hot skillet. Cook 2 minutes or until lightly browned. Remove from skillet.

4. Spread uncooked side of tortilla with cream cheese; arrange strawberries down center of tortilla. Roll up tortilla or fold to serve.

Makes 1 serving

Nutrients per Serving: Calories: 114, Calories from Fat: 21%, Total Fat: 3 g, Saturated Fat: 2 g, Protein: 5 g, Carbohydrate: 18 g, Cholesterol: 8 mg, Sodium: 256 mg, Fiber: 7 g, Iron: <1 mg, Calcium: 51 mg, Vitamin A: 62 mg, Vitamin C: 28 mg, Sugar: 4 mg.
Dietary Exchanges: ½ Fruit, 1 Starch, ½ Fat

Mango Vanilla Parfait

½ (4-serving size) package
    vanilla sugar-free
    instant pudding mix
1¼ cups fat-free (skim) milk
½ cup mango cubes
2 large strawberries, sliced

3 sugar-free shortbread
    cookies, crumbled *or*
    2 tablespoons reduced-
    fat granola
Strawberry slices for
    garnish

1. Prepare pudding according to package directions using 1¼ cups milk.

2. In parfait glass or small glass bowl, layer quarter of pudding, half of mango, half of strawberries and quarter of pudding. Repeat layers in second parfait glass. Refrigerate 30 minutes.

3. Just before serving, top with cookie crumbs and garnish with strawberries. *Makes 2 servings*

Tip: If you haven't tried fresh mango, you have a treat in store when you taste this lush tropical fruit. Look for fruit that is firm but not hard. Let mangoes ripen in a paper bag at room temperature until they yield slightly to pressure and have a heavenly fragrance.

Nutrients per Serving: Calories: 153, Calories from Fat: 9%, Total Fat: 1 g,
Saturated Fat: 1 g, Protein: 6 g, Carbohydrate: 29 g, Cholesterol: 3 mg,
Sodium: 129 mg, Fiber: 2 g, Iron: <1 mg, Calcium: 199 mg, Vitamin A: 295 RE,
Vitamin C: 29 mg, Sugar: 18 g
Dietary Exchanges: 2 Starch, ½ Milk

Easy Citrus Berry Shortcake

1 individual sponge cake
1 tablespoon orange juice
¼ cup lemon chiffon sugar-free, nonfat yogurt
¼ cup thawed frozen fat-free nondairy whipped topping

⅔ cup sliced strawberries or raspberries
Mint leaves (optional)

1. Place sponge cake on serving plate. Drizzle with orange juice.

2. Fold together yogurt and whipped topping. Spoon half of mixture onto cake. Top with berries and remaining yogurt mixture. Garnish with mint leaves. *Makes 1 serving*

Nutrients per Serving: Calories: 173, Calories from Fat: 7%, Total Fat: 1 g, Saturated Fat: <1 g, Protein: 4 g, Carbohydrate: 37 g, Cholesterol: 39 mg, Sodium: 116 mg, Fiber: 3 g, Iron: 1 mg, Calcium: 74 mg, Vitamin A: 24 RE, Vitamin C: 64 mg, Sugar: 9 g
Dietary Exchanges: 1 Fruit, 1½ Starch

Easy Citrus Berry Shortcake

Peach Custard

½ cup peeled fresh peach or
  nectarine cut into chunks

1 can (5 ounces) evaporated
  skimmed milk*

¼ cup cholesterol-free egg
  substitute

1 packet sugar substitute *or*
  equivalent of
  2 teaspoons sugar

½ teaspoon vanilla

Cinnamon

*If a 5-ounce can is not available, use ½ cup plus 2 tablespoons evaporated skimmed milk.

1. Preheat oven to 325°F. Divide peach chunks between two 6-ounce ovenproof custard cups. Whisk together milk, egg substitute, sugar substitute and vanilla. Pour mixture over peach chunks in custard cups.

2. Place custard cups in shallow 1-quart casserole. Carefully pour hot water into casserole to depth of 1-inch. Bake custards 50 minutes or until knife inserted in center comes out clean. Remove custard cups from water bath. Serve warm or at room temperature; sprinkle with cinnamon.　　*Makes 2 servings*

Note: Drained canned peach slices in juice may be substituted for fresh fruit.

Nutrients per Serving: Calories: 52, Calories from Fat: 2%, Total Fat: <1 g, Saturated Fat: <1 g, Protein: 5 g, Carbohydrate: 7 g, Cholesterol: <1 mg, Sodium: 71 mg, Fiber: 1 g, Iron: 1 mg, Calcium: 202 mg, Vitamin A: 117, Vitamin C: 3 mg, Sugar: 7 g
Dietary Exchanges: 1 Fruit

Cinnamon Compote

½ cup unsweetened
   pineapple juice
⅛ teaspoon ground
   cinnamon

1½ cups cubed cantaloupe
½ cup blueberries

1. In small saucepan combine juice and cinnamon. Cook and stir over low heat 4 to 5 minutes or until slightly syrupy. Cool slightly.

2. Combine cantaloupe and blueberries. Pour juice mixture over fruit; toss. Refrigerate until cold. *Makes 2 servings*

Nutrients per Serving: Calories: 98, Calories from Fat: 4%, Total Fat: 1 g, Saturated Fat: <1 g, Protein: 2 g, Carbohydrate: 24 g, Cholesterol: 0 mg, Sodium: 14 mg, Fiber: 2 g, Iron: 1 mg, Calcium: 28 mg, Vitamin A: 390 RE, Vitamin C: 62 mg, Sugar: 21 g
Dietary Exchanges: 1½ Fruit

Blueberry Custard Supreme

½ cup fresh blueberries
2 tablespoons all-purpose flour
1½ tablespoons granulated sugar
⅛ teaspoon salt
¼ teaspoon ground cardamom

¼ cup cholesterol-free egg substitute
1 teaspoon grated lemon peel
½ teaspoon vanilla
¾ cup reduced-fat (2%) milk
1 teaspoon powdered sugar

1. Preheat oven to 350°F. Spray 1-quart soufflé or casserole dish with nonstick cooking spray. Distribute blueberries over bottom of prepared dish.

2. Whisk flour, granulated sugar, salt and cardamom in small bowl. Add egg substitute, lemon peel and vanilla; whisk until smooth and well blended. Whisk in milk. Pour over blueberries.

3. Bake 30 minutes or until puffed, lightly browned and center is set. Cool on wire rack. Serve warm or at room temperature. Sprinkle with powdered sugar just before serving.   *Makes 2 servings*

Blackberry Custard Supreme: Substitute fresh blackberries for blueberries; proceed as directed.

Nutrients per Serving: Calories: 155, Calories from Fat: 11%, Total Fat: 2 g, Saturated Fat: 1 g, Protein: 7 g, Carbohydrate: 27 g, Cholesterol: 7 mg, Sodium: 249 mg, Fiber: 1 g, Iron: <1 mg, Calcium: 117 mg, Vitamin A: 56, Vitamin C: 7 mg, Sugar: 18 g
Dietary Exchanges: ½ Fruit, 1 Starch, ½ Milk

Blueberry Custard Supreme

Cranberry Bread Pudding

½ cup day-old French bread
 cubes
1 tablespoon dried
 cranberries or tart
 cherries
⅓ cup fat-free (skim) milk
1 tablespoon refrigerated
 cholesterol-free egg
 substitute

1 tablespoon brown sugar
¼ teaspoon vanilla
⅛ teaspoon ground
 cinnamon

1. Preheat oven to 350°F. Toss together bread cubes and cranberries. Place in 6-ounce custard cup.

2. Stir together milk, egg substitute, brown sugar, vanilla and cinnamon. Pour over bread mixture. Bake 22 to 25 minutes or until knife inserted in center comes out clean. Cool slightly.

Makes 1 serving

Nutrients per Serving: Calories: 163, Calories from Fat: 5%, Total Fat: 1 g, Saturated Fat: <1 g, Protein: 6 g, Carbohydrate: 33 g, Cholesterol: 1 mg, Sodium: 151 mg, Fiber: 1 g, Iron: 1 mg, Calcium: 150 mg, Vitamin A: 146 RE, Vitamin C: 7 mg, Sugar: 17 g
Dietary Exchanges: 1½ Starch, ½ Milk

Berries with Banana Cream

⅓ cup reduced-fat sour cream

½ small ripe banana, cut into chunks

1 tablespoon frozen orange juice concentrate

2 cups sliced strawberries, blueberries, raspberries or a combination

Ground cinnamon or nutmeg

1. Combine sour cream, banana and juice concentrate in blender. Cover and blend until smooth.

2. Place berries in two serving dishes. Top with sour cream mixture. Sprinkle with cinnamon. *Makes 2 servings*

Nutrients per Serving: Calories: 135, Calories from Fat: 25%, Total Fat: 4 g, Saturated Fat: 3 g, Protein: 4 g, Carbohydrate: 23 g, Cholesterol: 13 mg, Sodium: 29 mg, Fiber: 4 g, Iron: 1 mg, Calcium: 78 mg, Vitamin A: 60, Vitamin C: 87 mg, Sugar: 19 g
Dietary Exchanges: 1½ Fruit, 1 Fat

Raspberry Smoothies

1 cup plain nonfat yogurt
   with aspartame
   sweetener
1 cup crushed ice
1½ cups fresh or frozen
   raspberries

1 tablespoon honey
2 packets sugar substitute *or*
   equivalent of
   4 teaspoons sugar

1. Place all ingredients in food processor or blender; process until smooth. Scrape down sides as needed. Serve immediately.

Makes 2 servings

Nutrients per Serving: Calories: 143, Calories from Fat: 4%, Total Fat: <1 g, Saturated Fat: <1 g, Protein: 8 g, Carbohydrate: 28 g, Cholesterol: 2 mg, Sodium: 88 mg, Fiber: 6 g, Iron: 1 mg, Calcium: 145 mg, Vitamin A: 230 RE, Vitamin C: 42 mg, Sugar: 31 mg.
Dietary Exchanges: 1½ Fruit, ½ Milk

Index

Notes

METRIC CONVERSION CHART

VOLUME MEASUREMENTS (dry)

1/8 teaspoon = 0.5 mL
1/4 teaspoon = 1 mL
1/2 teaspoon = 2 mL
3/4 teaspoon = 4 mL
1 teaspoon = 5 mL
1 tablespoon = 15 mL
2 tablespoons = 30 mL
1/4 cup = 60 mL
1/3 cup = 75 mL
1/2 cup = 125 mL
2/3 cup = 150 mL
3/4 cup = 175 mL
1 cup = 250 mL
2 cups = 1 pint = 500 mL
3 cups = 750 mL
4 cups = 1 quart = 1 L

VOLUME MEASUREMENTS (fluid)

1 fluid ounce (2 tablespoons) = 30 mL
4 fluid ounces (1/2 cup) = 125 mL
8 fluid ounces (1 cup) = 250 mL
12 fluid ounces (1 1/2 cups) = 375 mL
16 fluid ounces (2 cups) = 500 mL

WEIGHTS (mass)

1/2 ounce = 15 g
1 ounce = 30 g
3 ounces = 90 g
4 ounces = 120 g
8 ounces = 225 g
10 ounces = 285 g
12 ounces = 360 g
16 ounces = 1 pound = 450 g

DIMENSIONS

1/16 inch = 2 mm
1/8 inch = 3 mm
1/4 inch = 6 mm
1/2 inch = 1.5 cm
3/4 inch = 2 cm
1 inch = 2.5 cm

OVEN TEMPERATURES

250°F = 120°C
275°F = 140°C
300°F = 150°C
325°F = 160°C
350°F = 180°C
375°F = 190°C
400°F = 200°C
425°F = 220°C
450°F = 230°C

BAKING PAN SIZES

Utensil	Size in Inches/Quarts	Metric Volume	Size in Centimeters
Baking or Cake Pan (square or rectangular)	8×8×2	2 L	20×20×5
	9×9×2	2.5 L	23×23×5
	12×8×2	3 L	30×20×5
	13×9×2	3.5 L	33×23×5
Loaf Pan	8×4×3	1.5 L	20×10×7
	9×5×3	2 L	23×13×7
Round Layer Cake Pan	8×1½	1.2 L	20×4
	9×1½	1.5 L	23×4
Pie Plate	8×1¼	750 mL	20×3
	9×1¼	1 L	23×3
Baking Dish or Casserole	1 quart	1 L	—
	1½ quart	1.5 L	—
	2 quart	2 L	—

Savor over 50 good-for-you recipes that serve just one
or two. Bursting with flavor, these diabetic recipes
prove that a special diet doesn't have to be dull.

◆ Satisfying dishes for
everyday dinners and
casual entertaining

◆ Great-tasting meatless
recipes for delightful
change-of-pace meals

◆ Streamlined recipes with
only five ingredients

◆ Boldly flavored recipes that
wake up your tastebuds

Manufactured in China.

◆ Simply sensational desserts
that are a snap to prepare

ISBN 0-7853-7659-3   Publications International, Ltd.